GOD'S TROUBADOUR

GOD'S
TROUBADOUR

The Story of Saint Francis of Assisi

by SOPHIE JEWETT

with paintings by Giotto

NEW YORK
THOMAS Y. CROWELL COMPANY

The publishers wish to thank the Basilica Patriarcale e Sacro Convento di S. Francesco, Frati Minori Conventuali, at Assisi and the Church of Santa Croce, Florence, for the reproduction of the Giotto frescoes; and Fratelli Alinari, Florence, and D. Anderson, Rome, for the photographs of these frescoes. The photographs on pages 55 and 107 are by Alinari; the others are by Anderson.

CONTENTS

PAINTINGS

These paintings are reproductions of the Giotto frescoes portraying the life of Saint Francis of Assisi. They are all located in the Church of San Francesco, Assisi, except for "The Vision of the Crucifixion," which is in the Church of Santa Croce, Florence.

GOD'S TROUBADOUR

He prayeth well, who loveth well
Both man and bird and beast.

He prayeth best, who loveth best
All things, both great and small;
For the dear God who loveth us,
He made and loveth all.

COLERIDGE

A CHILD OF
LONG AGO

UNDER THE arched gate of a city wall, a group of people stood watching the road that wound down the mountain and off across the plain. The road lay dusty and white in September sunshine, and the eyes of the watchers followed it easily until it hid itself in a vast forest that filled half the valley. On the point where road and forest met, the sharpest eyes were fixed.

The crowd was gay, but not noisy. There were few words and long silences, as always when people are waiting and expecting. Among all the eyes that watched the sunny road that day, the most earnest were those of Madonna Pica Bernardone, and the merriest were those of her little boy Francis, for the company was gathered to see the homecoming of Messer Piero Bernardone, the richest merchant of Assisi, and the lady Pica was his wife, and little Francis was his son.

The others were friends and neighbors of Piero. Some were rich customers, who wondered if the merchant had found for them the beautiful stuffs which they had ordered. Certain of the company were only idlers, glad enough to break the dullness of the long, warm afternoon.

1

Assisi, at whose gate the watchers stood, lies far across the sea in beautiful Italy. It is a little city, built on a mountainside, with a great wall all about it, and a castle on the height above, and it looks very much as it did on that September afternoon more than seven hundred years ago, when Francis Bernardone waited for his father. Inside the walls, the stone houses are crowded together, making narrow, crooked streets, so steep, often, that no car can drive through them. Some streets, indeed, are simply long flights of stone steps, where the children play, and the patient donkeys climb up, carrying heavy loads of charcoal or faggots.

But, though the streets are narrow, Assisi is not gloomy. Everywhere there is sunshine and bright color. Above the brown tiled roofs rise tall green cypress trees; over a bit of garden wall trail red trumpet-creepers and blue morning-glories; even the window sills are gay with pink and red geraniums. In the open square the market gardeners sell ripe grapes and plums and figs, covered with vine leaves to keep them fresh.

Outside the city gates, all the world seems like a fair garden. The hillsides are covered with olive trees, whose gray leaves twinkle like silver when the wind blows through them. Some of the trees look almost as old as the city walls, for their trunks are only hollow shells through which one sees the blue sky, though their tops still bear fruit bravely every year.

AN UMBRIAN TOWN AND CHURCH

From the foot of the mountain stretches the river valley, bright with wheat fields and tall corn, and vineyards where the vines hang in heavy garlands from one mulberry tree to another. Between the rows of trees, in the shadow of the vines, great white oxen move slowly, dragging clumsy, old-fashioned ploughs; and down a sunken road that cuts through vineyards and cornfields go strong, brown peasant women with burdens on their heads.

Little Francis Bernardone must have trotted up and down the same steep streets, and have played in the same squares

3

that one sees today; but the valley over which he looked, on this autumn afternoon, contained fewer vineyards and corn-fields, and far more forest trees. Francis wondered what might lie hidden in the forest, for he had never traveled beyond the place where the white road disappeared.

The hour grew late, and the tired watchers shaded their eyes from the low sun that shone across the valley from the western mountains. Suddenly Francis shouted aloud, and, in a minute, the shout was taken up by many voices: "He is coming! He is coming!" They saw, at first, only a cloud of dust, moving along the road; but soon horses and riders could be discerned, in a long line, half-hidden by the dust that rose in their path and turned to gold and crimson haze in the sunset.

As the horsemen climbed the hill to the city gate, the sight was more like the coming of a prince than of a merchant. Piero Bernardone rode ahead, in a company of soldiers, well armed and mounted upon fine horses. Behind this group followed a train of pack-horses and mules, heavily loaded with the rich goods that the merchant was bringing home. Last of all came another band of soldiers, some mounted, some on foot.

All this escort was customary for a rich merchant in those days, for the roads were often held by wandering bands of soldiers or highway robbers. Piero Bernardone needed many swords to defend the silks and velvets, gold embroideries and

4

jewels which he had bought in the great market towns of France and northern Italy.

At the gate of Assisi, Piero Bernardone dismounted gravely. He kissed the Lady Pica and the little Francis; he greeted his friends, somewhat coldly, perhaps, for he was a proud, hard man; but he turned a second time to kiss his boy, whom he loved dearly. Then Francis knew the proudest minute of his little life; for he was mounted upon his father's horse, while Piero and the Lady Pica walked beside him, and all the company, talking eagerly, entered the gate of San Pietro, and wound slowly up the stony streets that led to Piero Bernardone's home.

Inside the house, that night, Francis listened with wide eyes to his father's stories, for the merchant had always interesting adventures to tell. He had visited the great fairs, to which other merchants came, from Greece, from Africa, from Syria, from Germany and England. While he bought and exchanged goods, he heard news from all over the world, a world in which news traveled slowly, for there were no newspapers, nor telegrams, nor railroad trains.

On his way homeward the merchant was a welcome guest at the castles of knights and princes. Noble ladies bought his silks and laces, famous warriors begged him for tidings of war in other lands, and all listened to any new stories which he had learned on his journey.

5

Of all the merchant's hearers none was so eager as his son Francis. For him the stern Piero remembered all the strange and beautiful tales that he heard by the way; stories of Charlemagne and Roland; of King Arthur and his Knights of the Round Table. For him he learned the gay songs of the wandering poets, Troubadours, as they were called, who sang in the courts of kings and in the halls of nobles. Their songs were of brave knights in shining armor, and of ladies with white hands, beautiful eyes and sweet, unforgettable names.

Piero Bernardone cared little for the courtly words of these Troubadour songs, but, as he listened, he remembered the clear, childish voice at home, always quick to repeat new verses and new melodies. So Piero was glad when he heard the same song many times of an evening; and, next day, in the saddle, while he thought of prices and profits, his rough voice sang, over and over, daintily fashioned rhymes in praise of Isoline and Blanchefleur, of Beatrice and Amorette.

Francis learned all the stories and all the songs. Especially he loved the adventures of King Arthur and Sir Gawain, Sir Tristram and Sir Lancelot. On this September evening he listened till his big eyes were dim with sleep, and all night long he dreamed of becoming a great man, not a merchant like his father, but a knight like Lancelot.

6

THE YOUNG
TROUBADOUR

AS FRANCIS BERNARDONE grew
from a boy to a man, he made friends with a company of gay
youths, the sons of the greatest and richest families of Assisi.
Their fathers were counts, and dukes and princes, and the
lads were vain of the names they bore, and of the palaces
where they lived. It was a lawless company, bent on having a
good time, and thinking nothing of the comfort of other
people. The pranks of these young nobles were so reckless

and, sometimes, so wicked that the good people of Assisi lived in terror of what they might do next.

The youths welcomed Francis into their fellowship because, though he had not a noble name, he had splendid clothes to wear, and much money to spend; and because, among them all, no one laughed so merrily or sang so sweetly as the merchant's son. The hours always went more gaily when Francis was of the party, for it made one feel happy just to look at his bright face.

Piero Bernardone was proud that his son should be the friend and pet of these young lords, but the lad's gentle mother grieved that her kind-hearted little boy should come to be a wild and wicked man. Her heart ached in the night, when the noisy group went laughing and shouting through the streets, and she could hear the voice of Francis, sweeter and louder than the rest, singing a bit of Troubadour song that he had learned as a child:

> *My heart is glad in springtime,*
> *When April turns to May;*
> *When nightingales sing in the dark,*
> *And thrushes sing by day.*

The mother would listen till the laughter and singing were far away and faint, and the last sound was always the voice of her boy, which, indeed, she seemed to hear long after all was silent in the narrow street. When the neighbors complained that the conduct of the boys was too bad to be endured, the merchant only laughed. "It is the way of the world," he said. "Francis is no worse than the others. Boys must be boys. What would you have?"

But his wife would speak softly, with tears in her gentle eyes: "Wait, I have great hope that he will yet become a good Christian." The mother knew all that was best in the boy. She thought: "However careless and wild he may be, he has a kind and loving heart." And she was right. In his gayest moments Francis was always quick to pity anyone who was poor or in pain.

But one who is thoughtless is always in danger of being cruel. One day a man, ragged and hungry, crept in at the open door of Piero Bernardone's shop. Piero was absent, but Francis was spreading out beautiful silks and velvets before two customers, for he sometimes sold goods for his father. Standing in his dirty, brown rags among the red and purple stuffs and the gold embroideries, the beggar cried: "In the name of God, give me something, for I am starving!"

Francis, whose mind was intent on his bargain, impatiently sent the man away. A moment later, he was sorry. "What would I have done," he said to himself, "if that man had asked me for money in the name of a count or baron? What ought I to do when he comes in the name of God?" Leaving

9

the astonished customers in the shop, the boy ran out into the street, found the beggar and gave him all the money he had in his purse.

Despite his gay life, Francis had times of being thoughtful, and dissatisfied with himself. As he went up and down the streets of Assisi, well dressed and well fed, he saw people sick and hungry and ragged, glad to receive a crust of bread or an old cloak. "These people," thought Francis, "would live for months on the money that I waste in one day." Sometimes he would throw his purse to a starving man, or his bright cloak to a ragged one, and his merry friends would laugh and jest at him for his folly. Then they would all ride away gaily, and even Francis would forget.

He did not forget his old love for the stories of King Arthur and the Round Table. He disliked more and more the thought of being a merchant. He wanted to travel, to see faraway countries, but he wanted to go as a soldier, not as a tradesman. He wanted to storm great castles, to ride at the head of a fearless band of knights.

He loved the knights of the old stories, not alone because they were gracious in speech, true of their word, and kind to all the unfortunate and weak. Perhaps it was his love for

BROTHER FRANCIS GIVING HIS CLOAK TO A POOR MAN

gentle manners and brave deeds that kept Francis from becoming altogether hardhearted and selfish in these days.

Besides the songs of love and of battle, he had learned wise little verses about the duties of knighthood, and sometimes, when he and his friends had been most rude and unknightly, the old rhymes came back to his mind like a reproachful voice:

> *Nowhere is such a noble name*
> *As that of chivalry;*
> *Of coward acts and words of shame*
> *It is the enemy;*
> *But wisdom, truth, valor in fight,*
> *Pity and purity,*
> *These are the gifts that make a knight*
> *My friend, as you may see.*

12

THE YOUNG SOLDIER

THERE WERE many and terrible wars
in Italy in the thirteenth century, and the chance of trying
his fortune as a soldier was not long in coming to Francis
Bernardone.

Only fifteen miles away from Assisi stands a larger city,
called Perugia. It also is built upon a mountain, and the two
towns seem to smile at each other across the green valley.
But for hundreds of years there were only bitter looks and

hatred between the two. Perugia, higher and stronger, lay like a dragon, ready to spring upon her small but furious enemy. Assisi, like a lion's cub, was always ready to fight. Sometimes the lion was victor; always it was fierce enough to make the huge dragon writhe with pain.

When Francis Bernardone was about twenty years old, there was war between the great dragon and the little lion. Down from one mountain came the Perugian army. Down from the other came that of Assisi. With the army of Assisi rode Francis and most of the company of friends who had been so merry together in times of peace. They were gay as ever, and eager to see what a real battle might be like.

The armies met in the plain, and fought by the riverside, near a tiny town called Ponte San Giovanni, the Bridge of St. John.

This time the Perugians were too strong for the Assisians, and the young soldier's first combat was a defeat. One day taught him all the horror of a field of battle. He saw men wounded and dying. He heard the terrified cries of riderless horses. He suffered from blinding sun and parching thirst. War, that he had thought so noble and glorious, seemed somehow confused and cruel and hideous.

The army of Assisi lost heavily that day. Many men were slain, many were made prisoners, and one of the prisoners was Francis Bernardone. He was too tired, too hungry and too thirsty to feel anything keenly except the need of sleep and food; yet he wondered how it had all happened. Could he be the same man who had gone about for days delighting in the song of a warlike Troubadour:

> *Luck to the arm that's quickest,*
> *And, if at odds ye strive,*
> *Die where the field is thickest,*
> *But never yield alive.*

He knew that he had not been a coward. He had not even been afraid, yet here he was unarmed and captive.

Because of his beautiful dress, and because of his courtly manners, Francis was placed, not among the common soldiers, but among the nobles. For a whole year he was a prisoner of war. It must have been a sad change from the free, wild life in Assisi. Captives, even if of noble rank, were not softly treated in old times; and, though Francis and his companions may not have suffered serious hardships, the long confinement was, in itself, a cruel thing to bear.

On Francis Bernardone, however, his misfortune sat lightly. The army of Perugia could not make a captive of his fancy. His fellow-prisoners were astonished to hear him tell of his hopes and plans for the future; of the battles he should fight; of the fame he should win; of the beautiful ladies who should smile on him. The brave knights whom

15

he admired, Gawain, Tristram and Lancelot, had sometimes fallen into prison, but had won their way out again, to fight better than before.

So Francis still dreamed of war and glory, and boasted in his pride: "You will see that, some day, all the world will adore me."

Though he was proud and boastful, Francis was still gentle-hearted, and quick to feel sympathy for all who were unhappy. Among the prisoners of war was one man so vain and ill-tempered that his companions would have nothing to do with him. The unfortunate creature sat gloomily apart, with a black frown on his face, and with black thoughts in his mind. The songs and jests and games with which the others whiled away the long hours made him seem all the lonelier in his silent corner.

The sight of the sad, bitter face was more than Francis could bear. Many times he slipped away from the noisy group of his comrades to speak cheerily to the solitary knight, and, little by little, with the friendliness that no one was ever known to resist, he won the heart of the miserable man. Through the good will of the boy whom everybody loved, the victim and his tormentors in the end became friends once more, and there was peace in the great prison.

All through the long winter, from across the valley, the sad eyes of the Lady Pica watched the towers of Perugia. In her heart she questioned what might have been her boy's fate. Was he ill, and suffering and lonely? When would he come back to her? She seemed still to hear him singing, as on the morning when he had ridden out so blithely to his first battle:

> *Comrades, let each be ready*
> *To give and take his part;*
> *Shields bright and lances steady,*
> *And all men glad of heart.*

If the breeze that swept down the long valley from Perugia could have carried the prisoner's merry voice, the mother might have been somewhat comforted.

In prison or out of it, the heart of Francis of Assisi was always the heart of the poet, the Troubadour. Because his companions remembered gratefully the songs and laughter that brightened their captivity, the story of his gaiety has come down to us across seven hundred years.

TO ARMS!

AT LAST there came a day when the prisoners were set free and Francis could return to his home. The wide valley, with its shining rivers, the far blue mountains and the green forest road must have been welcome to eyes that, for a long year, had looked at the world through prison windows.

We may be certain that Piero and Pica Bernardone were watching for their son, and that all the neighbors made merry

18

at his coming. We know that his gay young friends received him joyfully and that the old life of feasting, drinking and rioting began again.

Perhaps, in his delight at being free once more, Francis was more reckless than ever. At any rate, it is certain that, a short time after his return to Assisi, he suddenly became seriously ill. When, after long days of illness, he began to crawl about slowly, weak and pale, and leaning upon a stick, he was strangely unlike himself. Instead of being happy to be out of doors again, instead of frolicking with his friends, he was silent and sad at heart.

He wondered why he cared so little for the feasts and games and songs that he had delighted in only a few weeks before. Now, they did not interest him. It seemed to him that a man ought to have something better to do than simply to eat and drink, and wear fine clothes.

Because of his own pain and feebleness he felt sorrier than ever before for the lame, and blind, and the hungry beggars who came to his door, and his only pleasure was in giving them money and clothes and food.

As he listened to the talk in the market place by day, and in his father's house at evening, he heard many stories of the wars. Men told how houses were burned, fields and vineyards trampled and ruined; how women and children and helpless old men were killed, or left to die of hunger and cold. When he lay sleepless at night, he seemed to see again the battlefield of San Giovanni, and the faces of cruel men attacking, and of miserable victims wounded and falling. In these hours Francis doubted if war could be the glorious thing it had always seemed to him.

But when his friends began to tell him of new fighting in the south of Italy, and of a company of soldiers who were going from Assisi to join the army of a famous knight called Walter of Brienne, all was changed. The old love for battle and glory woke up in his heart, and Francis made haste to grow strong again that he might be ready to go to war.

These were exciting days for the invalid. The color came back to his cheeks and his eyes danced with joy at sight of the rich clothes he was to wear, the beautiful horse he was to ride, the bright shield he was to carry.

He forgot that he was but a page, and that his first fight had ended in defeat. He dreamed of winning great battles; of marrying a beautiful princess; of living in a magnificent palace, or riding to the wars at the head of knights and soldiers of his own.

Assisi was full of noise and battle in these days. Companies of soldiers rode through the narrow streets so recklessly that the folk on foot hurried into doorways, and stood open-mouthed with fear while the riders passed.

In the market place men talked in eager groups. The voices

were loud and excited, but louder still rang out the sharp blows of hammer on anvil, for every smith who knew how to make or to mend armor was busy from morning to late at night.

Furnaces stood in the open square, where the fires looked pale in the sunshine. Gay esquires brought from their masters bent or broken pieces of fine wrought steel, common soldiers brought their own clumsier armor; and the small boys of the city stood in admiring circles about the sounding anvils, and thought that, next to being a soldier, one would like to be a smith.

All this hurry of preparation was strong medicine to Francis. He forgot that he had been sick. He forgot that war had ever looked an evil thing to him. With his friends he was once more the gayest of companions, and he needed no urging to sing to them, to their hearts' content. Over and over he sang:

> *I love the gay spring weather,*
> *And all the trees a-flower,*
> *When a hundred birds together*
> *Make music every hour;*
> *But it sets my heart a-beating*
> *To see the broad tents spread,*
> *And bright-armed warriors meeting,*
> *And banners floating red.*

21

When camp and street are stirring;
   When the city gates stand wide;
When bands of knights are spurring
   Through all the countryside.

I know a joy that's dearer
   Than food, or drink, or rest,
When the battle-shouts come nearer,
   When flash bright sword and crest;
When above the trumpet's braying
   And shrill cries of distress,
I hear the mournful neighing
   Of brave steeds riderless.

Francis seemed to have become more boastful and more gay than ever, so that even his friends wondered at him, and asked him laughingly: "What is it that makes you so merry?" and he answered proudly: "I know that I am going to be a great prince."

Vain as he was, however, Francis never quite forgot that brave deeds and not fine garments make a good soldier. Among the company of knights who were going from Assisi, there was one who had for years been a great fighter, but who had suffered misfortune, and was now so poor that his clothing was actually ragged. To him Francis gave his own new coat and mantle, and the other accepted the gift quite simply, knowing that rich clothes are worth little, but that kind hearts are worth much.

When the good-bys were said and the horsemen clattered out of the city gate, no heart in all the company was so light as that of Francis Bernardone.

His mother watched him with grave eyes, remembering how many times she had seen the towers of Perugia fade into the red sky at sunset, and had prayed that her boy might come back to her. Now, he was going again, not to Perugia, but far to the south, to a country that she had never known. She wondered how he could smile at her so gaily as he rode away.

THE NEW ROAD

FRANCIS and his fellow soldiers were to spend the first night in Spoleto, a city about twenty miles south of Assisi, on the way to Rome. The road ran along at the foot of the mountain, sometimes through forests of oak and beech and walnut trees, sometimes between olive orchards and vineyards. Presently it struck across the plain to Foligno, a busy Umbrian town lying in the valley by the River Topino.

24

In the square of Foligno, Francis had often stood with his father, selling goods at the fairs. Today he held his head high as he rode through the familiar market place. He thought: "I shall come back a famous soldier, and I will never, never sell things at the fair again." He blushed with pride when someone in the street pointed him out to a companion, saying: "That young man, who is dressed and mounted like a lord, is the son of Messer Piero Bernardone, the merchant."

At Foligno the company halted to eat and drink, and to rest through the hottest hours of the day. When they were in the saddle again, and had left the city gates behind them, Francis no longer rode superbly, with his chin in the air. Instead, he went silently, with drooping head, and let his horse lag behind the others along the level stretch of road.

He could not himself have told what was the matter; nothing had happened; the woods were as green and the sunshine as bright as in the morning, but he who had been so proud and gay a few hours earlier felt strangely weary and sick at heart.

He lingered to let his horse drink from the clear, little river, Clitumnus, that comes dancing down from the mountain and glitters across the plain, but not even the song of the water made him merry. His comrades noticed his silence, but they were all too deeply interested in their own plans and hopes to think of anything else.

25

In the late afternoon they entered the glorious oak forest that filled the ravine where Spoleto lies at the end of the Umbrian Valley. Beyond, their way would be through a narrow mountain pass where, over and over again, armies had fought fiercely to hold the road to Rome. Deep in the cool woods, the birds were singing, and, for the first time in his life, it seemed to Francis that they sang not joyfully, but sadly.

Perhaps he had not grown strong after his long illness, and so could not bear the fatigue of the hard saddle ride. Whatever the reason may have been, it is certain that, when the party reached Spoleto, Francis took to his bed with fever, and that his companions rode on, next day, without him.

And Francis had no wish to follow them. As once before, but this time more powerfully and surely, there had come upon him a great horror of a soldier's life. As he lay burning with fever and sleepless with pain, all his dreams of glory faded. Instead of knights, with shining armor and bright banners, he seemed to see women weeping, little children begging for bread, beautiful cities ruined and desolate.

We do not know how he made his way home. It was a strange and sorry journey, and, at the end of it, he met with ridicule from those who had seen him ride away so bravely to seek his fortune as a soldier. But if his thoughtless friends mocked him, and his father and brother reproached him, his mother was glad to welcome and to care for him. Perhaps she, alone, understood the change in him.

The first days after his return were the most sorrowful that Francis had ever known. Though he was sure that he had decided rightly, it pained him sorely to know that his friends thought him weak, or, perhaps, even cowardly. Besides being hurt, he was puzzled, not knowing what he ought to do next. A week ago his path had lain clear before him, like the white road in the valley; now it had lost itself in a tangled forest.

We do not know how long his trouble lasted, nor what he was doing in these dreary weeks; but we know that, by and by, he began to see plainly again, and all his doubts and puzzles vanished. It was as if he had found his way through the forest and saw the path that he must take, a narrow path and rough, a lonely path, but straight to follow.

He did not know that in a few years hundreds of fellow travelers were to come and ask that they might walk with him along that narrow way; that instead of being, as he had dreamed he might, Francis Bernardone, the most famous knight in Italy, he should become Brother Francis, the man whom all men loved.

All that Francis knew was that, in the place of his old love for a soldier's life and his old desire to become a great prince, had come a new love and a new desire: a love for all the ragged and hungry and sick and sorrowful folk in the world, and a desire to feed, and clothe, and heal and comfort them all.

This new feeling was very different from his former pity for the poor. He had always been pitiful and generous, glad to give gifts like a patron; now he was like a lover, with a love that seemed to him big enough to include everybody in Assisi, everybody in the wide world. And Francis was happy again. His friends who had seen him, after he came back from Spoleto, pale and sick, restless and disappointed, saw his face brighten, and heard him singing as of old. "Francis Bernardone is like himself once more," they thought.

But when they found that he no longer cared for their suppers and their games, they said: "How stupid he is!" and they left him to go his own way.

"THE OTHER LIFE IS
AS MY LIFE"

Who gives himself with his alms, feeds three,
Himself, his hungering neighbor, and Me.

LOWELL

ABOUT THIS time Francis made a
journey to Rome. Perhaps his mother hoped that a change
would bring back his strength; perhaps Piero hoped that,
seeing many people and hearing news of the war, his son
might again be fired with soldierly ambition. Francis himself

29

longed to see the city where so many saints and martyrs had lived and died, and where, he thought, he should find wise and holy men to tell how he might carry out his wish to help and heal all the misery in the world.

It was strange to him to travel again over the road to Spoleto, yet he was far happier in spirit than on that earlier journey. South of Spoleto, the way was new to him, though he came to know every foot of it a few years later.

In the thirteenth century, as in the twentieth, all travelers to Rome were eager to visit the Church of St. Peter, but in the thirteenth century the church itself was not the one whose vast dome we see today. It was an older church that Francis Bernardone sought out, but it stood on the same spot, and it must have been exceedingly beautiful. To Francis it seemed the most sacred place in the world, as he walked up the great nave, between the long rows of columns, and as he knelt to pray before the altar.

But when he stood again in the church porch, he noticed the crowd of wretched, dirty human beings who clamored for alms, pulling at the garments and crying in the ears of all who entered the door. As he looked at them and listened to them his eyes filled with tears, and all the sunshine seemed to fade out of the bright Roman sky.

"What does it mean?" he asked himself. "Here, in Rome, where there are so many men rich, and wise, and holy, is there no one who will take care of all these miserable creatures?"

In the shade of a column, a little apart from the others, a beggar was crouching who neither cried to the passers-by, nor clutched at their cloaks. He only stretched out a thin hand, and looked wistfully up into their faces. Francis stood long watching this man. No one gave to him, no one seemed even to see the huddled figure. The beggar's face looked weary and hopeless, and from time to time the thin hand dropped to his knee.

Still Francis watched. He forgot all about the crowds of people. He forgot everything. He was wondering what it must be like to sit from morning till night, ragged and weary, begging for one's daily bread.

Suddenly, acting as he always did on the moment's impulse, Francis spoke to the silent beggar and led him away to a deserted corner at the further end of the portico. He gave the man a piece of money and, with no explanation, proposed to exchange clothes with him. The beggar stood stupefied as Francis began to pull off his own rich cloak. It may be that he thought the boy a criminal trying to disguise himself; it may be that he thought him mad. Whatever he thought, he was glad enough to trade his tattered beggar's dress for clothing such as he had sometimes fingered, wonderingly, but had never even hoped to wear.

What became of the man we do not know, but Francis, wrapped in a tattered, dirty cloak, went back, to sit all day long, begging at the door of St. Peter's church.

Perhaps it was a foolish thing to do, but, at any rate, the hunger and weariness of that strange day made Francis understand better than he ever had before the suffering of the poor. And because he understood, he was the better able to help.

After this one day of a beggar's life, Francis was sure that no service in the world could be too low for him to do gladly, and no human being too revolting for him to touch. The most hideous cripple by the roadside seemed to him friend and brother, and his only grief was that he could not make them all understand his love and sympathy.

This joy and confidence lasted all through his journey home. Spoleto was not gloomy this time, and the birds in its oak woods sang to him merrily. As he came up the familiar Umbrian Valley, until he met the little river Tescio on its bright, zigzag way, Monte Subasio stood above Assisi rose-red in the sunset, and the walls of the city shone like transparent glass, looking to the eyes of Francis like the walls of the New Jerusalem.

In the weeks that followed, it seemed to Francis that simply loving his fellow men made all life joyous and easy; but one day he discovered that there were still battles to fight.

32

He was riding across the valley toward Assisi, and neared a little hospital for lepers, where he had often stopped with gifts of money. His heart was full of sorrow for these sufferers from the most terrible of all diseases, and he thought: "I will go in, today, and leave something for them."

Outside the gate of the hospital, crouched against the wall in the sunshine, one of the lepers sat to ask alms of passing travelers. The poor man was covered with sores, and revolting to look upon. At sight of him, Francis felt a sickening sense of disgust and horror. He drew his purse hastily from his belt and, tossing it to the leper, rode on as fast as his horse could carry him, trying to forget the pale face that had been raised to his.

Suddenly, like an arrow, the thought struck him: "That man, also, is my brother, and I have despised him!" He dropped his rein, and the horse went slowly along the rough road between the olive orchards.

Francis was both ashamed and disappointed. He said to himself: "My purse was an insult, for I gave it without love, and with more scorn than pity."

The spring sun was high and hot; the sky was cloudless; not a shadow lay on the vast, bare height of Monte Subasio. At a fountain beside the road some women were washing. They sang as they worked and, at the end of the long fountain basin, a group of children shouted with laughter, dipping

33

their little hands into the cold water, and splashing one another merrily. All the world seemed happy in the sunshine, and, by contrast, the misery of the poor leper seemed the greater.

At the sound of hoofs, the songs and laughter ceased and all turned to look at the newcomer; but, to the surprise of everyone, the horseman wheeled swiftly about, and clattered back in the direction from which he had come. "Who is he?" one woman asked of another. "Only that young Bernardone, the merchant's son," was the answer; "people say that he has gone mad."

Then an old, bent woman spoke: "Mad or not, he has a kind heart. It was his gold that kept my poor Giovanni alive last winter. I wish that more of the rich folk were mad like him."

Francis heard nothing. He rode fast across the valley toward the little hospital. He had not been gone ten minutes, and the leper, scarcely recovered from his surprise at the generous gift he had received, was creeping to the gate with his treasure. He moved slowly, as if in pain. Francis sprang from his horse, and, kneeling in the dusty road, he lifted the leper's hand to his lips and kissed it, as he had been taught to kiss the hand of a bishop or a prince.

It is likely that the leper was as greatly puzzled as the beggar in the porch of St. Peter's had been, but Francis

Bernardone was not mad. Instead, he had learned, through his own failure and shame, a lesson that some men never learn; for, "though I give all my gifts to feed the poor, and have not love, it is nothing."

From that spring morning, at the gate of the leper hospital, until the day of his death, Francis of Assisi never met the man who was too filthy, or too loathsome, or even too wicked, for him to love.

FATHER AND SON

TO FRANCIS, the world seemed full of new and beautiful things to do. When he saw a poor little chapel by the roadside, he wanted to bring stones and build it up with his own hands. When he saw an old woman bending under a heavy load of faggots, or grass from the mountain, he wanted to take the burden upon his own shoulders. When he saw a hungry child, he wanted to give it his own dinner. Above all, it seemed to him that he must go everywhere and

36

tell people to love and help each other, instead of fighting with swords and lances.

Piero Bernardone had been willing to give his son money and clothes and horses, that the boy might be as gay as any of his young friends; but Piero did not like to have his money thrown away on all the poor folk of Assisi.

Before many days, Francis found that he had not much of his own to give. He did have some beautiful pieces of silk and velvet and embroidery that his father had brought him from one of his long journeys. One day Francis took these out from the carved oak chest in which he kept his treasures. He spread them upon the floor and looked at them with the trained eye of a merchant's clerk. He knew exactly how much money they ought to bring.

The next morning he rolled his merchandise into a parcel, bound it to his saddle, and rode away to Foligno, to the market place, for it was the day of the fair. The square was thronged with people. Under gay booths in the center, all along the streets, against the palace walls, even on the steps of the cathedral, buyers and sellers were bargaining. Many were there who had seen Francis ride gallantly by, a few months before, on his way to the war. Now, they were astonished to see him, with simple clothes and gentle manner, offering his goods for sale.

When all the gay stuffs were gone, Francis sold his horse

37

also, and started back toward Assisi on foot, with a full purse at his side. Perhaps the horse he had just sold was the very one on which he had ridden so merrily over the same road with his soldier friends.

However that may be, as Francis neared home and turned off from the high road, to climb the stony footpath that shortens the way, his heart was far happier than it had ever been before. He smiled to himself as he remembered how he had loved war; how his heart had delighted in banners and bright armor and martial music. Now, he had no sword nor shield, not even a horse, and he was a most unsoldierly figure with his dusty feet and his plain clothes.

On the hillside, he turned and looked down the road once more, wondering what had become of the knightly company who had gone to do battle in the far-off south. As he went on his way again he thought gladly, "Though He was only the Carpenter of Nazareth, my Captain is greater and braver than any Crusader. I can be a soldier still!"

The time came quickly when Francis needed more than a soldier's courage. His father and his brother were very angry with him, because, they said, he was making himself and the family ridiculous. Piero Bernardone had always been a hard man, and now, in his wrath and disappointment, he was cruel. The poor mother tried to make peace, but Piero only became as angry with her as with his son.

38

At one time Francis hid himself for days in the little chapel of San Damiano, outside the city, where he had found a friend in the poor priest. Piero sought for him in fury, but did not find him. Francis could not long endure to be in hiding, like a coward, and he determined to go home to his father, and to explain that he must live the life that he knew to be right.

By this time all Assisi had heard of the trouble between father and son, and there were many people who thought Francis a madman. Before he reached his father's door the idlers and children were shouting about him, making so much noise that Piero burst into the street, to know what was happening.

When he saw Francis he was wild with anger. He would not listen to a word, but fell upon the youth like a savage. The crowd stood back in horror, and the father with cruel blows and crueler curses dragged his son away and thrust him, half strangled, into a dark room and locked the door.

How long Francis was kept a prisoner we do not know. At last his father was obliged to go away on a journey, and Lady Pica, who saw that all her efforts to soften her husband's heart were fruitless, unlocked the door and set her son at liberty.

All Piero's fatherly love had turned to bitter hatred. When he came home, he went to the rulers of the city and demanded that Francis should be banished from Assisi. Then Francis appealed for protection to the bishop, to whom he told the whole sad story. He told him of his past life and of the life he now wished to lead; he told him of his father's anger and of his mother's grief.

One day, in the little square in front of the bishop's palace, there was a strange scene. Before a crowd of men and women and children, who wondered at the change in the boy they had always known, and who wondered still more at the fierce anger of the father, Francis stripped off the clothes he wore and laid them, with the little money that he had left, at the bishop's feet.

Then he spoke, and his voice rang clear and sweet, with no touch of fear or of anger: "Listen, all of you, and understand. Until this time I have called Piero Bernardone my father, but now I must serve God. Therefore I give back to my earthly father all my money and my clothing, everything that I have had from him, and from this time forth I shall say only: 'Our Father who art in Heaven.'"

The crowd of neighbors and friends stood silent and astonished to see the merchant greedily seize the money and the garments and go away without one look of pity for his

BROTHER FRANCIS GIVING UP EARTHLY GOODS

40

son. Then Bishop Guido, with his own cloak, covered the lad, who stood trembling, partly with cold and partly with grief.

We must remember that Francis had a loving, gentle spirit and longed to be at peace with his father; but, as he had said himself, he was Christ's soldier, and a soldier has no choice but to obey. In his heart he seemed to hear quite plainly his Captain's order: "If you are to be my soldier, Francis, you must be poor, not rich; you must not wear soft clothing nor feast at princes' tables; but you must go through city streets and country lanes, and take care of my sick folk and my poor."

"LADY POVERTY"

The olives they were not blind to him,
The little gray leaves were kind to him
When into the wood he came.

SIDNEY LANIER

AFTER THESE things, Francis found himself without home, or clothing or money. Scantily clad in an old cloak, lent to him by the bishop's gardener, he wandered outside the city gate on the mountainside. It was early spring, and the snow lay white in the ravines above

43

him, and on all the far-off peaks across the valley. But the sky was blue and, on the stony slopes, the yellow broom was in full flower.

Francis threw himself down on the sunny side of a great olive tree. He leaned against the warm gray trunk, and looked and listened. A tiny lizard darted across the ground close to his hand, and shot up the tree like a green flame. The wind in the dry, silvery olive leaves whispered like a kindly voice, and in every thicket the birds were singing.

It seemed to Francis that the wind spoke to him, and that the birds sang to him. He forgot his sorrows and sang also the gay old Troubadour songs, which were the only ones he knew. He did not sing battle songs, but those that told of April, of nightingales, of roses and of fair ladies. Like a courtly minstrel he sang:

> *O nightingale, go where my lady dwells,*
>   *And bear her news of me;*
> *Then listen while she truly tells*
>   *Her tales to thee;*
> *And she, if she doth not forget*
>   *My love and pain,*
>   *Will bid thee swiftly turn again*
> *Where I wait yet*
>   *To know how pass my lady's days,*
>   *To learn of all her words and ways.*

44

The nightingales had not yet come from the South, but the sparrows made merrier than ever in the bright broom, and a wood dove, hidden in an oak tree, was calling to his mate; and Francis sang again, the song that he had loved best in the days when he dreamed of fighting splendid battles for the sake of a golden-haired princess:

> *Great lady, who art fairest*
> *Men say, of all things fair,*
> *The noble name thou bearest*
> *None may so fitly bear;*
> *Clear fountain of all beauty*
> *That gladdens the green earth,*
> *Thy deeds of love and duty*
> *Are more than blood and birth.*

Even as he sang, he thought: "The Lady whom I shall serve has no other suitor, no poet has ever sung her praises, and no knight has ever fought her battles; for I will be the faithful lover of the Lady Poverty, whom all men else despise."

Little by little the good people of Assisi became accustomed to seeing Francis Bernardone dressed in a dust-colored robe, with a cord about his waist. He went barefooted and bareheaded. Many still thought him mad, and the street children shouted at him and threw mud and stones. The young men, with whom he had eaten so many suppers and sung so

45

many songs, now jeered at him, and even his brother joined in the cruel sport.

Francis was too tender-hearted not to be hurt by all this, but he never answered angrily. He thought: "It is because they do not understand."

But, if his rich friends were unkind, the poor folk who had loved him for his gentle words and for his gifts, when he was the proud young merchant, loved him the better now that he had given them all his money, and was ready to share his crust of bread with any hungry man. At the little hospital where Francis had gone first in splendid clothes, with a full purse at his side, the lepers wondered to see him come so poorly dressed, with no horse and no money. But, when they saw how gently he took care of those who were most sick and helpless, they called him "Brother Francis"; and they forgot their suffering while he talked and sang to them.

One by one new friends came to Francis asking that they might live as he lived, wear a coarse robe and go barefooted, and work with him for the poor and the sick. The first was a former friend, a rich gentleman of Assisi, named Bernardo di Quintevalle. This man gave away his riches and came to live with Francis in the service of the Lady Poverty. He was called Brother Bernardo, and Francis loved him dearly. Because he was the first of the little company of Brothers, Francis called him "my oldest son."

The second of the new friends was named Piero, and the third Sylvester. Sylvester had been a selfish man, greedy of gold, but when he saw Francis and Bernardo give away their wealth so gladly, and live so happily without it, he wanted for himself that joy that his money could not buy, and he ended by coming to be one of the Brothers.

When there were several in the company of Brothers, Francis named them "The Little Poor Men of God." Three of them who were most with Francis afterward wrote down the story of his life. These three were Brother Egidio, Brother Ruffino and Brother Leone. Brother Leone's name means Lion, but he was so gentle and so unlike his name that Francis used to call him "God's Little Lamb." Of Brother Egidio, who loved long, dangerous journeys, and who was always ready for any adventure, Francis would say: "He is one of the knights of my Round Table."

The new Brothers were without money, and without even a house in which to live. In the summer it seemed to them to matter little. They slept out under the wide sky, as the shepherds still sleep in Italy, and the moon, rising over Monte Subasio, flooded all the valley with white light; and the nightingales filled the forest with wonderful music. But when the autumn nights grew cold, when the moonlight fell upon a valley thick with mist, the little company of Brothers looked about for shelter.

47

Their refuge was a little building, scarcely more than a hovel, falling to ruin, and abandoned. It had once been a retreat for lepers, but the lepers had been moved to that hospital nearer the city which Francis had so many times visited. The older building was called Rivo Torto, Crooked Brook, from the little stream beside which it stood.

Here the Brothers lived all through the winter, and, when spring came, so many had joined the Brotherhood that they had not room to sleep. Miserable as it was, Francis and his first Brothers loved their little hovel, and were happy there, and from its scant shelter they went out to carry joy and healing to the sad and to the sick.

The ruined hospital long ago disappeared, and today it is not easy to find even the place where it stood. Among fields, where the corn grows so tall that one walks as if in a forest, there is a tiny chapel with an old well and a hut or two. Even the name has been changed, and if one asks a peasant the way to Rivo Torto, he will point out a great church far away; yet, in spite of years and changes, the memory of Francis and his little Brotherhood still shines over the spot, warm and bright, like the August sunshine on the corn.

Straight across the plain, not far from Rivo Torto, in the midst of tall forest trees, stood a little chapel where Francis and his few Brothers often went to rest and to pray. A rich abbot, seeing that the Little Poor Men had no place to sleep, made them a present of this chapel and the ground about it. Here they built rude huts and planted a hedge and made for themselves a home, which they called the Portiuncula, the little portion. A great church, called Santa Maria degli Angeli, has been built upon this spot and the little old chapel still stands under its dome.

The life of the Poor Brothers does not seem a gay one, as we read about it, yet they were happy-hearted. There was no work too humble nor too hard for them to do. They helped at ploughing in the spring, at reaping and threshing in the summer. In autumn they gathered grapes or nuts, and in winter olives, for in Umbria the olive harvest is in the winter. When the Brothers were paid for their work, they gave away everything except what was needed for the day's food.

They often made long journeys, working their way from place to place. Thus it happened, one day, that Brother Egidio, the "Knight of the Round Table," was standing in a public square in Rome, when a countryman came by, asking for a laborer to go and gather nuts from a very tall tree.

The men who stood about said: "No: we remember your tree. It is too high and we do not want to break our necks."

"I will go, gladly," said Egidio, "if you will give me half the nuts I gather."

The bargain was made, and Brother Egidio climbed to the highest branches and beat down all the nuts. His share he gathered up in his robe, and went merrily through the streets of Rome, giving nuts to the poor folk whom he met, till all were gone.

Wherever the Little Poor Men came they brought help and comfort, and people came to love them and to welcome them, even those who, at first, had mocked at them and thrown stones. For love and joy and helpfulness and gentle words make most of the happiness of life, and all these gifts the Brothers had to give, even when they had not a penny, nor a loaf of bread.

THE BIRD SISTERS

THE BROTHERS who knew Francis best in these years, who shared his joys and sorrows, and even his thoughts, have many stories to tell of his love for flowers and birds and animals. When they were planting their little pieces of ground around the poor huts in the plain, he used to bid them leave a corner of good earth for "our little sisters, the flowers." Once, in the market place of Siena, he rescued a pair of doves from being sold. He gathered them up in his

51

robe, saying: "Little sister-doves, you are simple, and good, and pure. Why have they captured you? I will save you from death and make you nests for your little ones."

There is a pretty story of the friendship of Francis with a family of red-throats who used to come and pick up crumbs on the table where the Brothers were eating. Another story is of a frightened hare which someone had caught in a trap. "Come to me, Brother Hare," said Francis, and the trembling little beast fled to him and let itself be caressed by his kind hands. It even refused to run away, on being set down, so that Francis was obliged to carry it into the woods and leave it free to find its way home.

One day Francis was in a little boat, being ferried across the lake of Rieti, when a boatman made him a present of an uncommonly large fish, just caught and gasping for breath. The gift was accepted gladly, but in a minute the astonished giver saw Francis drop the creature back into the water, bidding it thank God. Probably neither the fish nor the fisherman understood the tender heart that could not bear to see anything suffer pain; yet, doubtless, in its own way, the poor fish was grateful to swim in the cool water again, and it is to be hoped that it kept away from nets and hooks forever after.

With birds Francis felt himself always among dear and happy friends. But one time these little companions were too noisy in their merrymaking. It was on a day when Francis stood up to speak to a great crowd of men and women gathered out of doors. Hundreds of swallows were wheeling all about, as one often sees them on a spring afternoon, twittering and calling with shrill voices while they hunt their supper on the wing.

This time the birds flew so low, and were so many and so loud, that Francis could not make himself heard. Suddenly he turned from his audience and spoke into the air: "It is time that I should have my turn to talk, little sister Swallows," he said; "be quiet and listen until I have finished"; and, so says the old story, the swallows obeyed his voice.

A short time after, Francis went on his way toward Bevagna, a small town on the southwestern side of the Umbrian Valley. Looking off from Assisi, one may still see the road by which he must have walked. Two or three of his Brothers were with him, but Francis was not talking. His head was bent and he seemed to be thinking so hard that he had forgotten all about his comrades.

Suddenly, as it is written in an old book called *The Little Flowers of St. Francis,* "he lifted up his eyes and saw many trees along the side of the road and in their branches an almost countless number of birds; so that Francis wondered, and said to his companions: 'Wait for me here, and I will go and preach to my sisters the birds.' And he went into the field and began to preach to the birds that were on the ground, and, quickly, those that were up in the trees came to him, and they all kept quiet while Francis finished his sermon, and, even then, they did not go away until he had given them his blessing. And, when Francis went among them touching their heads, not one of them moved.

"The substance of the sermon that Francis made was this: 'My bird sisters, you are much beloved by God your Master, and always, in every place, you ought to praise Him, because He has given you liberty to fly everywhere; and He has given you also clothing double and triple. You are loved also by the air which He has given to you; and moreover, you neither sow nor reap, and God feeds you, and gives you the rivers and the fountains to drink from; He gives you the mountains and the valleys for your refuge, and the tall trees for your nests, and, although you do not know how to spin nor sew, God clothes you and your children. God must love you much, since He gives you so many blessings, and therefore, be careful, my sisters, of the sin of ingratitude, and always seek to praise God.'

"While Francis said these words, all those birds began to open their beaks, and stretch out their necks, and spread their

BROTHER FRANCIS PREACHING TO THE BIRDS

wings, and bend their heads reverently toward the earth, and, with acts and songs, they showed that the Holy Father gave them great pleasure. And Francis rejoiced and made merry together with them, and he wondered much at such a multitude of birds, and at their beauty and at their attention and tameness, and he devoutly thanked God for them."

The old story goes on to tell how, after the sermon, the great flock of birds rose into the air with wonderful songs and flew away north and south and east and west, even as the Poor Brothers must go, who, like the birds, had nothing of their own, but depended only on God's care of them.

This story of the birds was so much loved and so often told that, years afterward, the painters often painted it on the walls of the churches. You may still see, in the great Church of St. Francis in Assisi, a picture by the painter Giotto, of the gray-robed Brother, standing among the birds, and telling them, so simply that it really seemed as if a bird might understand, of the Father without whose love not even a sparrow falls.

One night Brother Francis and Brother Leone, "God's Little Lamb," were alone together. It was May, and in a great ilex tree near them a nightingale was singing sweet and clear, in the stillness. To Francis the song seemed all joy and praise. "Come, Brother Leone," he cried, "let us sing, too, and see which will tire first, our voices or that of the

56

nightingale." But Brother Leone, who was, perhaps, tired and sleepy, excused himself, saying that he had no voice.

Then Francis, his heart filled with the gladness of the beautiful springtime, went out into the darkness, and, all night long, the man and the bird sang wonderful songs of love and praise. But even God's Troubadour could not outdo the little unseen singer in the ilex tree, and, at last, Francis owned merrily that Brother Nightingale was victor in this strange singing match.

BROTHER WOLF

THE HUTS in the plain below Assisi were the home of the Little Poor Men, in so far as they had a home; but, like the Troubadours and Knights Errant, they were wanderers always. Just as Sir Lancelot or Sir Gawain would ride away from the court of King Arthur to fight for any forlorn lady or for any hard-pressed knight, so Brother Leone or Brother Francis would set forth at any moment to carry help to the miserable.

But the Brothers went on foot, and they wore no armor, and fought no battles; yet they had need to be as brave as the best of knights, for they went among the sick, and cared for

58

those who were dying of most terrible diseases. They met fierce enemies, too, since many people hated them because they spoke without fear in the streets, saying that pride and greed and war are wicked, and that folk should live by love and labor, not by fighting and robbery.

When people saw that the Brothers really lived as they preached, that, when they were stoned by cruel hands and abused by cruel tongues, they returned only gentleness for anger, many began to listen gladly, and even barons and princes came to love Francis and his Brothers, as the poor and wretched had loved them from the first.

Francis himself had a manner so sweet and winning that no one could refuse to listen to him; and sometimes he used to be sent for to make peace between two enemies, because even angry men, listening to his voice, forgot their hatred, and were ready to forgive and to be friends again. The stories say, moreover, that he could control not fierce men only, but the fiercest of wild beasts.

One of the places which Francis often visited is a little city called Gubbio, about fifteen miles north of Assisi. Almost all the way the road lies across the high mountains and the traveler can overlook the long Umbrian valley. From these bare heights, Perugia and Assisi seem to lie low, but far to the south, on clear days, the tops of the tallest Apennines stand out against the sky. Before the road drops to the narrow valley which lies below the gates of Gubbio, Francis, who loved the mountains, always turned to look back at the great peaks, shining white in wintertime, or soft and blue if it were summer.

Gubbio looks not unlike Assisi, but is still more steeply built up a mountainside. In those days the stone houses seemed to huddle within the great city walls for shelter, for there was frequent fighting at Gubbio. Even in times of peace, people were often afraid to go beyond the gates, because in the forests and caves on the mountain lived daring robbers and brigands. Besides the savage men, there were also savage beasts, and the shepherds feared for their lambs and kids, when they heard the howling of the wolves at night.

Once, when Brother Francis came to Gubbio, all the city was in terror because of a wolf, the largest and fiercest ever known. The huge creature prowled about the country, devouring sheep and goats; but, worse than that, it fell upon men, and had killed more than one shepherd. No man dared to go out of the gates alone, and even three or four together went armed, as if to battle; for the beast came close to the city walls, and his strength was as that of three hunters.

Bands of citizens had been out to seek the wolf, but had found only the track of his big feet, and the bones of the victims that he had eaten. Every night the folk of Gubbio, safely barred within their stone houses, told a new story of the four-footed enemy: how a shepherd had lost his fattest sheep and two of his best dogs; how a soldier, riding alone, toward evening, from the next town, had seen a great gray creature moving in the woods by the roadside, and had spurred his horse to its best speed and reached the gate with the beast close at the heels of the frightened horse.

Night after night the children of Gubbio shivered in their beds, thinking of a long shadow that crept about the city walls in the moonlight, and seeming to hear the pad of four swift feet, coming nearer and nearer.

Brother Francis had been often in Gubbio and was well known there, and much loved, and therefore all the people turned to him with the stories of their suffering. He was sorry, says the old tale, to see the folk wishing, but not daring, to go outside the gates, because the wolf was most terrible and fierce. To the astonishment and horror of everybody, Francis declared that he would himself go out and meet the wolf.

Though all the crowd begged him not to venture, and filled his ears with accounts of the cruelty of the beast, the Little Poor Man, followed by one or two Brothers, went out from the city gate and down the road toward the spot where the wolf was thought to lurk. Behind the Brothers came the citizens of Gubbio, still frightened, but curious to see what would happen, and, it may be, quieted by the coolness and

61

fearlessness of Francis. Close at the heels of the Brothers marched certain venturesome boys, and at the very end of the procession dangled a group of smaller, timider children, round-eyed and open-mouthed, who clutched each others' hands, and were always ready to scamper home at a moment's warning.

About a quarter of a mile beyond the gate, where a wood of tall oaks and walnuts shadowed the road, those who were nearest turned pale at the sight of the wolf, coming swiftly along, with his great jaws open, eager to spring upon Brother Francis, who walked ahead and alone. He went, not as a soldier goes to meet an enemy, but as one might go out to meet a welcome friend.

As the unarmed man and the wild beast neared each other, Francis called, cheerily: "Come hither, Brother Wolf! I ask you, for Christ's sake, to do no harm to me nor to anyone."

Then the crowd saw, with wonder, that the terrible wolf stopped running, and that the great, wicked jaws closed; and, presently, the creature came softly up to Brother Francis and, meek as a lamb, lay down at his feet. And Francis spoke to him as one man might reason with another: "Brother Wolf, you do much harm in all this countryside, and you have committed many crimes, hurting and killing God's creatures. Not only have you killed and eaten beasts, but you have dared to kill men, made in God's image, and, therefore, you deserve

62

to be punished like the worst of thieves and murderers; and all the people cry out and murmur against you; and everybody is your enemy."

The wolf lay perfectly still, with his head flat in the dust of the road, and his red tongue lolled out like that of a winded hound. The people forgot their fright, and spread themselves in a circle that all might see and hear; the children tiptoed closer, to look at the monster who had filled all their dreams with terror.

"But I wish, Brother Wolf," went on the voice of Francis, "to make peace between you and this folk, so that you shall not harm them any more; and they shall forgive you all your misdeeds, and neither the men nor the dogs shall trouble you any longer."

Then, with body and head and tail, the great wolf seemed to agree to all that Brother Francis said.

Perhaps the wolf wondered what he should do for dinner, if he could not kill a sheep or a child; perhaps he was so charmed by this strange, gentle voice that he forgot all about his dinner. Brother Francis did not forget, as his next words showed. "Brother Wolf," said he, "since you are honestly willing to make and keep this peace, I promise you that, as long as you live, the men of this place shall give you food, so that you shall never go hungry; for I know well that it is hunger that has made you do all this evil. But I want you to promise me, in return, that you will never harm any human being, nor any animal. Will you promise me this?"

The wolf nodded his head, as if he said: "I promise."

And Francis said: "Brother Wolf, I want you to make me so sure of your promise that I cannot doubt it." The man held out his hand, and the beast lifted his paw and laid it clumsily on Brother Francis' palm, as much as to say: "Here is my hand, I will keep my part of the treaty."

"And now," said Francis, "I wish you, Brother Wolf, to come with me, and not to be afraid, and we will finish this business."

Francis turned back toward the city, and the wolf walked beside him like a pet lamb; and the people of Gubbio followed, in great wonder, silently. But, once within the city, they spread the news from street to street and everybody, big and little, young and old, crowded into the square to see Brother Francis and the wolf.

Beside the fountain, in the center of the square, stood the Little Poor Man in his gray gown, with the great gray beast at his side. When he spoke, his clear voice carried far, and all the crowd fell silent, striving to hear. "Listen, my friends," said Francis, "Brother Wolf, who is here before you, has promised me on his honor never to hurt you again in any way; and you, in your turn, must promise to give him all that he needs. I will go surety for him that he will keep his

64

promise." And all the people, with one voice, pledged themselves to feed the wolf, and not to harm him.

Then, before them all, Brother Francis said to the wolf: "And you, Brother Wolf, promise again before all this people that you will keep faith with them, and will hurt no man, nor animal, nor any living thing."

The wolf knelt down and bent his head and said, as well as he could, with his body, his head and his ears, that he meant to keep his word. And Brother Francis said: "Give me your hand here, before all the people, as you did outside the gate."

The big gray paw was laid again in the hand of Brother Francis, while all the people shouted to heaven for joy that God had sent so good a man to deliver them from so terrible a beast.

After this Brother Wolf lived in Gubbio, and went about tamely from door to door, even entering the houses, without doing harm or being harmed. He was well fed and politely treated by everybody, and not a dog dared to bark at him. He must have led a long life of evildoing before his change of heart, for, at the end of two years, he died of old age. When he died, all the citizens of Gubbio mourned for him greatly, for his own sake, and because the sight of him walking so meekly through the streets had made them always remember the goodness of Brother Francis.

THE THREE ROBBERS

BROTHER FRANCIS made many journeys through the mountains and valleys about Gubbio. All the people, rich and poor, came to know the drooping gray figure and the face that was always so cheerful and kind, though often it looked pale and thin.

One of the little cities where he used to visit is called Borgo San Sepulcro. It lies at the foot of a mountain, and outside its walls was a deep moat with a drawbridge before

66

each gate, for a city on a plain is harder to defend in battle than a city on a hill. Today, the moat is dry and planted with vineyards, but the old walls are solid still, though they are so covered by trailing vines that an army of small boys might scale them.

From Borgo San Sepulcro, Brother Francis visited the little villages that lay, each at the gates of a great castle, as a dog crouches at his master's feet. For village and villagers belonged to the lord of the castle, and, though he might be cruel, and ill-treat them, they had no other protection in war save that of the castle courtyard, which was big enough to shelter them all.

One day, in a place called Monte Casale, about two hours' walk from Borgo San Sepulcro, a youth from one of the castles came to Brother Francis. He had a great name and great wealth, and the common people stood aside to let him pass.

The youth knelt down humbly before Francis and said: "Father, I wish to be one of your Poor Brothers."

Francis looked down kindly into the eager young face and replied: "My son, you are used to a beautiful home, to rich clothing and delicate food; how will you endure poverty and hardship such as ours?"

But the lad answered simply: "Can I not bear all these things, by the help of God, even as you do?"

Francis was greatly pleased by this answer. He joyfully received the youth into the company of Little Poor Men, giving him the name of Brother Angelo; and his trust in the new Brother was so great that, a little time after, he made him guardian of a small house, nearby, where some of the Brotherhood were living.

The house stood in a wild region of mountains and forests. At this time, three famous and terrible robbers lived in the woods, and were the terror of all the people of the neighborhood.

On a certain day, when Francis was absent, these men came to the house of the Brothers and asked for food. Brother Angelo answered them sharply, saying: "You cruel thieves and murderers! you are not ashamed to steal what others have worked to earn; and you even have the face to ask for that which has been given in charity to God's poor! You are not fit to live, since you reverence neither men nor yet God, who made you. Away with you! and do not let me see you here again!"

The robbers went off with dark looks and muttered curses, but Brother Angelo felt well satisfied with himself, and perhaps a little proud that he had been so good a guardian for the Brothers.

An hour later Brother Francis returned to the house, weary with long walking on the rough mountain paths. Over his shoulder he carried a bag of food that had been given to him for the Brothers and for their poor folk.

Brother Angelo greeted him with the story of the three robbers. He doubtless expected praise for having rid the house of such dangerous evildoers; but, to his surprise, Francis looked at him, sadly and sternly, and said: "My son, you have behaved most cruelly. One should receive sinners with gentleness, not with harshness, even as Jesus Christ, who said: 'They that are whole have no need of a physician, but they that are sick,' and 'I came not to call the righteous, but sinners to repentance.'

"Moreover, Jesus Himself used often to eat with the most wretched sinners, and you, my son, have forgotten all charity, and the teaching of Christ. Go then quickly; take this food and follow the robbers, as fast as you can, until you overtake them. When you find them give them this bread from me; and kneel down before them and confess your fault, and beg them, in my name, not to do any more evil. Tell them that, if they will give up their wicked life, I will find food for them always, and they shall want for nothing."

It was a hard minute for young Brother Angelo. He had looked for praise, and, instead, he was being reproved by the lips that had never before spoken any but gentle words to him. Surely this command was strange and unreasonable! How could he run after the men he had just driven away?

How could he, a Brother, ask pardon of such wretched men?

But as he looked into the face of Brother Francis, so stern, and yet so pitying, a thought that he had never known before stirred in his heart, the thought that it is possible to love not only those who are good and gentle, but even the wicked and vile. For it was easy to see that Francis loved and pitied these robbers, who were prowling about, not far away, hungry and fierce, like wild beasts. When this new thought came to Angelo, all his anger disappeared, and he was ready and glad to obey Brother Francis.

He threw the bag over his shoulder, and ran along, as fast as he could, by the narrow path that the thieves had taken. The way was steep and stony, but he did not notice. There had been a thunderstorm, but now the sun came out, and the wind piled the clouds white and high above the mountain tops, and the sky was deep blue. The sunshine seemed to Angelo like the face of Brother Francis, shining upon him and driving away all his hard and cruel thoughts.

He began to be more and more sorry as he remembered the rough words he had used to the beggars. As he went on, seeing no one, sometimes through the woods, sometimes over stony pastures, where sheep were feeding, he began to think: "Suppose I cannot find the men? Suppose they have taken some other road, and are wandering in the woods, hungry and miserable?" At the thought, he pulled the bag higher on

70

his shoulder, and hurried faster and faster along the path.

Just as the path made a sharp turn and entered the woods again, Angelo saw the three wretched men sitting under a chestnut tree, trying in vain to find a few nuts among the husks, for it was late autumn and the nuts were all gathered or decayed.

As Angelo came running along the path, the three robbers eyed him sullenly, and when they recognized the haughty youth who had driven them so harshly from his door, they were ready to fall upon him and beat him. A minute later they sat in speechless surprise, for the boy threw himself and his bag down before them, crying: "Here is food, my brothers, take it, and forgive my cruelty. Brother Francis sends me to you, and begs you, for his sake, to accept the food; and he bids me tell you that, if you will give up your wicked life, he will care for you and feed you always."

Perhaps there were never three men more astonished than the robbers of Monte Casale. They devoured the food greedily, for they were starving; but, as they ate, they began to say among themselves: "What miserable creatures we are, who live by thieving and murder, and fear neither men nor God! And here is this youth, who said to us only what we richly deserved, asking our pardon, and bringing us food, and promising that the holy Brother Francis will forgive and care for us!"

The three robbers became sorrier and sorrier as they remembered all their wicked deeds. By and by one of them said: "Let us go ourselves to Brother Francis and ask him if God will yet forgive us. It may be that the good Brother will help us to live like honest folk once more."

Thus it came about that the three infamous robbers of Monte Casale joined the company of Little Poor Men, and spent the rest of their days in doing good and not evil to their fellow men.

NURSE AND PATIENT

ONE DAY in summer, Francis of Assisi came out from the city gate and walked down the mountain on his way to the Portiuncula. He took a path that he loved well because it led him by the chapel of San Damiano, where, long ago, the good priest had hidden him from his father's anger, and where many times, in that first year of trouble, he had found shelter and comfort.

73

He loved the little chapel the more because he had helped to rebuild it. He knew the very stones that he had laid with his own hands. Now, the place was dear to him for another reason, for house and garden and little chapel belonged to a sisterhood, whose leader, Sister Chiara, had come to him in the early days at the Portiuncula asking that she might live the same life of poverty and service as that of the Little Poor Men. To her, and to all her company, Francis had been friend and father, and it made him happy that his old refuge had become their home.

From the gate of San Damiano Francis could see the whole valley, where the August air quivered with heat, and the river-bed lay white and dry. The little huts in the plain were hidden in deep forest, and he thought how cool the shadow of the oaks and tall walnut trees would be at the end of his journey. Hot as it was, he did not take the shortest road, but turned into a footpath that led to the leper hospital. He was barefooted and bareheaded; his robe was the color of the dusty path; he walked with bent head, wearily, for he was not strong, and the air at the foot of the mountain was still and close.

Under the trees, men and women were resting through the hottest hours, and the children were playing quietly. A baby lay sound asleep on the brown grass, where the shadow of broad vine leaves fell across its face. A tired-looking donkey nibbled sadly along the hedgerows, which were dry and dusty, for the August rains had not begun.

As Francis drew near, the men and women rose to greet him, and the children left their play to run and kiss his hand, for no one in all the countryside was so beloved as the Little Poor Man. He petted the children; he found a greener twig for the donkey, and called him "Brother Ass"; he lingered to ask and answer questions, for he knew all the peasants, and they told him all their joys and sorrows.

As he turned to go, a little girl, pushed forward by her mother, came toward him timidly, holding up a basket covered over with vine leaves. The sun shone on the child's curly head and tiny brown arms. As she lifted the basket higher the green leaves slipped aside, showing the deep purple of the August figs. "Will you accept them, Father, for your supper at the Portiuncula?" The mother said. "They are ripe and sweet." The child said nothing, but stood smiling up into the kind eyes of the Little Poor Man. Brother Francis took the basket and bent to kiss the giver. "God reward you, little one," he said. "I will carry the fruit to our sick brothers at the hospital."

One of the first duties which Francis had taught his Little Poor Men was the care of the lepers, and some of the Brothers always stayed in the hospital, and Francis himself went often to nurse and comfort the sufferers. On this August day, to his surprise, he found his Brother nurses worn and discouraged.

They turned eagerly to him, as always when they were in trouble, and they told him a sad story. "Father," said one of them, "do not be angry with us, nor think that we have been impatient and have forgotten our rule of humbleness and service. There is here a leper so wretched in mind and body that not one of us can help him nor even control him. He is in constant pain, and nothing gives him relief, and he is as bad in spirit as in body, for he shrieks and curses when we come near him, and his words are so wicked that we are afraid to listen."

"I will go to him," said Francis, and they showed him the bed where the leper lay, muttering curses still with his parched and swollen lips. "God give you peace, dear Brother," said Francis, as he stepped to the bedside.

"What peace can I have from God, who has taken away from me peace, and every other good thing, and has made me altogether miserable?" cried the leper. "I am in pain day and night, and these Brothers of yours do not care for me as they should; they have done nothing to help," he complained, bitterly.

BROTHER FRANCIS CARING FOR A SICK MAN

"I will take care of you, Brother," said Francis, "I will do for you whatever you wish."

"Then wash me from head to foot with your own hands," cried the leper, still angrily, "for all my body is covered with sores, and I am loathsome, even to myself."

Francis very patiently began to bathe the leper, and his hand and his words were so tender that the wretched man was soothed, and ceased to curse and complain. His pain vanished, too, under the care of his new nurse, and, as he became comfortable in body, he grew gentle in spirit, and was sorry for his unkind and wicked words.

The other Brothers were astonished to see the man who had given them so much trouble become gentle and patient and grateful to them all.

One day, as Francis sat by the bedside, the sick man turned to him with tears in his eyes. "Forgive me, Brother," he said, "all the evil that I have spoken of you and of your Brotherhood."

Francis took his hand and spoke softly to him: "My Brother, you have suffered great pain. If you have not borne it meekly, ask God to forgive you, for His love is greater, far, than ours."

The old story tells how, a few weeks later, the leper died, at peace with God and with all the world.

WITH THE
CRUSADERS

FROM THE first, the way in which the Brotherhood of Little Poor Men grew in numbers was a wonderful thing to see. Within a few years it had outgrown the settlement in the plain and was a vast company, like a great army sent out to make, not war, but peace. The groups of Gray Brothers were known all over Italy, and companies of them had gone to France and Spain and Germany, and even to the north of Africa. In foreign lands, just as in Italy, they

79

preached their simple Gospel, and preached it best by caring for the sick and the poor.

Sometimes the Brothers were received kindly in the far-off countries; sometimes they were mocked and stoned, as they had been at home, and in Africa a brave little band was cruelly put to death.

It seemed to Francis that he could not bear to stay where he was known and safe, while his Brothers were enduring danger, and even death, in strange lands. Moreover, his heart yearned over the ignorant and miserable everywhere, and he longed to tell in other places what he had told in Italy, that men should love each other and live at peace, and that food and clothing and money should be for all, not for the few. It was only the Gospel of the Carpenter of Nazareth, but men had forgotten His teaching, though they built great churches in His honor, and though they went to war in His name.

In the year 1219, one of the great wars called Crusades, or Wars of the Cross, was going on. The Crusaders were soldiers from Europe, who fought in the Holy Land to drive the Saracens away from Jerusalem, in order that the Holy

BROTHER FRANCIS RECEIVING THE RULES OF HIS
ORDER FROM POPE HONORIUS III

Sepulchre where Christ was buried, and the hill where He was crucified, might not be in the hands of unbelievers, for the Saracens were not Christians, but Mohammedans. They were brave and able soldiers, however, and many times the knightly armies from England, France, Germany and Italy suffered terrible defeats in Egypt or in Palestine.

Fifteen years earlier Francis Bernardone would have been the most eager of Crusaders. The thought of the long voyage, of the battles to be fought in Eastern lands for the rescue of the Holy Sepulchre, would have made him even happier than he had been when he rode out to his first fight. Now, Brother Francis, the Little Poor Man, was no less determined to go with the crusading army, but he went with only peace and pity in his heart. He knew that where there were battles there would be wounded and dying to tend and comfort, and he hoped that, in the midst of hatred and cruelty, he might find a chance to speak of love and gentleness. He even hoped that he might go among the armies of the enemy and preach to them.

The Italian Crusaders were to sail for Egypt from the port of Ancona, on the Adriatic Sea, toward the end of June. Francis and a company of his Brothers crossed the mountains from Assisi and reached Ancona in time to go about from ship to ship, seeking to find passage. Since they were not soldiers, and since they had no money, they were forced to trust to the friendliness of the ships' captains and, when the day of sailing came, places had been found for only Francis and eleven companions.

It was a sad minute, for all wanted to go, and Francis could not bring himself to decide whom to leave behind. As he walked with them along the white beach, and looked away over the blue harbor where the ships rode at anchor, he spoke sorrowfully: "My Brothers, the shipmen will not take us all, and I have scarcely the courage to choose between you. Let us seek to know what is God's will."

On the beach a little child was playing in the sand, and Francis called him to them. "Do you know numbers, little one?" he asked. "Can you count?"

"Yes, Father," the child answered, proudly, "I can count more than twenty."

Then count me out eleven of these, my Brothers, to go to sea with me tonight when yonder ships set sail."

The child did not understand what he was doing, but he went about solemnly among the company, and, with his small forefinger, told off eleven Brothers, and, at evening, these eleven sailed away with Francis and the Crusaders, across the southern sea.

On the water, the summer days were long and hot. Sometimes the wind died away, the sails hung empty, and the sun blistered the decks. The ships were crowded, and the soldiers

83

were uncomfortable and discontented. Many fell sick of sunstroke and fever, and Francis and his Brothers found plenty of misery ready to their kind hands.

At night, when the breeze freshened, and the great sails filled slowly; when the sky darkened and the stars came out; when the ship's prow and the long oars cut through waves of wonderful, shining light, all the wretchedness of the day was forgotten, and the voyagers made merry. The sailors sang at the ropes, the Crusaders, common soldiers and knights together, seated on the deck, listened while someone told a marvelous story of Tristram, or of Roland. Then a Troubadour would sing some brave or plaintive song, while his fingers made sweet music on an old Venetian lute.

Francis was soon known to all, and he found many new friends. Sometimes even the knightly tales were neglected, while the soldiers questioned the Little Poor Man and listened to the story of the Brotherhood of Assisi.

Francis was with the crusading army in Egypt for a long time, but we know little of what happened to him. A certain French bishop wrote home a letter which has, somehow, been kept all these seven hundred years. He tells in it of the wonderful "Brother Francis, whom everyone reveres because he is so lovable; and who is not afraid to go even into the army of the Saracens."

Francis was so fearless and so gentle that, usually, strangers

84

and even enemies received him kindly, and he came to be almost as well known among the Saracens as among the Crusaders. But there were some who hated him because he preached a strange religion, which they feared, thinking that it might bring success to the Christian armies and defeat to their own.

One day Francis and Brother Illuminatus, who was his comrade at this time, were returning alone from the Saracen camp to that of the Christians. Their course lay westward, and, where the treeless plain rose toward the red sunset, they could see the line of the Crusaders' tents. The distance was short, and they had good hope of reaching their friends before darkness fell, when, suddenly, from the south, a band of mounted men appeared.

As they came near, Francis could see that they were not Crusaders in heavy mail, but lightly armed Saracens, on swift Arabian horses. They swept across the plain like a flight of birds, and Francis watched them admiringly, for he loved all beautiful things. But the fleet riders had quick, fierce eyes. As they spied the gray robes, they wheeled sharply and fell upon the Little Poor Men, like wolves upon sheep, so the old story says.

Wounded and helpless in their cruel hands, Francis somehow made his enemies understand that he wished to be taken into the presence of the Soldan himself, their emperor.

Perhaps they were afraid to kill a man who appealed to them in the name of their master; perhaps they expected a reward for their prisoners; perhaps even their hard hearts were softened by the sight of men who neither fought nor feared. At any rate, they finally bound the two Brothers and carried them off to the Saracen camp. The next day Francis had his wish fulfilled, for he and Brother Illuminatus were brought into the royal tent.

The Soldan sat on a splendid throne, and his dress was rich and beautiful. All about the throne stood armed **guards,** and at the foot of it black Ethiopian slaves, with shining eyes and teeth. On one side were the Soldan's counselors, his Wise Men, who could read in the stars the things that were to happen in the future; who could tell the meaning of dreams, as the magicians had tried to do in Egypt, since the day, and long before the day when young Joseph put them all to shame.

The Wise Men wore turbans and long flowing robes. They had white beards, and deep-set eyes and solemn faces.

In front of the throne stood Francis and his one Little Brother. They were bareheaded and barefooted. Their rough gray robes were dusty and torn and stained with blood. They

seemed no match for the tall magicians, who looked down on them with scorn, thinking them madmen or fools. But the Soldan was grave and thoughtful. He wanted to know which of them spoke the truth, his learned counselors, whom he had always trusted, or these simple, poor men, with their new teaching.

The Wise Men could give no help to their Sovereign, and, at last, Francis said: "My lord, bid your slaves build here a fire before you, great and hot; it may be that God will show us a sign." When the red fire blazed high, Francis spoke across it to the magicians: "If you love your religion better than your life, walk into the midst of this fire with me, that it may be seen which faith should be held most certain and most holy."

The Wise Men cowered away from the flames with horror, and covered their faces in shame, knowing that they dared not go into the fire. And Brother Francis cried aloud to the Soldan: "Promise me, my lord, for thyself and thy people, that, if I come out unharmed, thou wilt worship Christ, and I will enter the fire alone."

But the Soldan was afraid, for he thought that his people might revolt, knowing that they held the Wise Men in great dread and honor. Therefore he hastily sent the Brothers, with a safeguard, back to the camp of the Crusaders; but he marveled much at the quiet gray-robed man who had no fear.

88

THE CHRISTMAS AT GRECCIO

The beautiful Mother is bending
    Low where her Baby lies
Helpless and frail, for her tending;
    But she knows the glorious eyes.

The Mother smiles and rejoices
    While the Baby laughs in the hay;
She listens to heavenly voices:
    "The child shall be King, one day."

O dear little Christ in the manger,
    Let me make merry with Thee.
O King, in my hour of danger,
    Wilt Thou be strong for me?

FROM THE LATIN OF JACOPONE DA TODI

THIRTEENTH CENTURY

ONE NIGHT in December, a few years after his return from the East, Brother Francis, with one companion, was walking through the beautiful valley of the Velino River, toward Rieti, a little city where he came often on his way from Assisi to Rome. Tonight he had turned somewhat aside from the main road, for he wished to spend Christmas with his friend, Sir John of Greccio.

Greccio is a tiny village, lying where the foothills begin, on the western side of the valley. The feet of Brother Francis knew the road so well that he could have walked safely in the darkness, but it was not dark. A full moon floated over the valley, making the narrow river and the sharp outlines of the snow-covered mountains shine like silver. The plain and the lower hills were pasture land, and, not far from the road, on a grassy slope, the Brothers saw the red glow of an almost spent shepherds' fire.

"Let us stop and visit our brothers, the shepherds," said Francis, and they turned toward the fading fire.

There was no sense of winter in the air, scarcely a touch of frost, and the only snow was that on the silver peaks against the sky. The shepherds, three men and one boy, lay sleeping soundly on the bare ground, with their sheepskin coats drawn closely around them. All about them the sheep were sleeping, too, but the solemn white sheep dogs were wide awake. If a stranger's foot had trod the grass ever so softly, every dog would have barked, and every shepherd would have been on his feet in an instant. But the dogs trotted silently up to the Gray Brothers and rubbed against them, as if they said, "We are glad to see you again," for they knew the friendly feet of the Little Poor Man, and they had more than once helped him to eat the bread that was his only dinner.

Followed by the dogs, Francis walked about among the shepherds, but they slept on, as only men who live out of doors can sleep, and Francis could not find it in his heart to waken them. The sheep lay huddled together in groups for more warmth. Around one small square of grass a net was stretched, and inside it were the mother sheep who had little lambs. There was no sound except the faint cry, now and then, of a baby lamb.

The coals over which the shepherds had cooked their supper paled from dull red to gray, and there was only a thin column of smoke, white in the moonlight. Francis sat down on a stone, and the largest of the white dogs pressed up against his knee. Another went dutifully back to his post beside the fold where the mothers and babies slept. The Italian hillside seemed to Francis to change to that of Bethlehem, which he had seen, perhaps, on his Eastern journey; the clear December night seemed like that of the first Christmas Eve.

"How these shepherds sleep!" he thought. "How they would awaken if they heard the 'Peace on earth' of the angels' song!" Then he remembered sadly how the armies that called themselves Christian had, year after year, battled with the Saracens over the cradle and the tomb of the Prince of Peace. The moonlight grew misty about him, the silver heights of the mountains and the silver line of the river faded, for the eyes of Brother Francis were full of tears.

As the two Brothers went on their way, Francis grew light of heart again. The sight of the shepherds sleeping on the grass had given him a new idea, and he was planning a surprise for his friends at Greccio. For at Greccio all were his friends, from Sir John, his host, down to the babies in the street. In the valley of Rieti he was almost as well known and as dearly loved as in his own valley of Assisi.

The children of Greccio had never heard of Christmas trees, nor, perhaps, of Christmas presents. I am not sure that, in the thirteenth century, Italians had the beautiful custom which they now have, of giving presents at Twelfth Night, in memory of the coming of the three kings with their gifts to the Christ Child; but in the thirteenth century, even as now, Christmas was the happiest festival of the year.

This year all the folk of Greccio, big and little, were happier than usual because their beloved Brother Francis was to help them keep their Christmastide. The next day Francis

92

confided his plan to his friend, Sir John, who promised that all should be ready on Christmas Eve.

On the day before Christmas, the people came from all the country around to see and hear Brother Francis. Men, women and children, dressed in their holiday clothes, walking, riding on donkeys, crowding into little carts drawn by great white oxen, from everywhere and in every fashion, the country folk came toward Greccio. Many came from far away, and the early winter darkness fell long before they could reach the town. The light of their torches might be seen on the open road, and the sound of their singing reached the gates of Greccio before them.

That night the little town was almost as crowded as was Bethlehem on the eve of the first Christmas. The crowds were poor folk, for the most part, peasants from the fields, charcoal burners from the mountains, shepherds in their sheepskin coats and trousers, made with the wool outside, so that the wearers looked like strange, two-legged animals.

The four shepherds who had slept so soundly a few nights before were of the company, but they knew nothing of their midnight visitors. The white dogs knew, but they could keep a secret. The shepherds were almost as quiet as their dogs. They always talked and sang less than other people, having grown used to long silences among their sheep.

Gathered at last into the square before the church, by

93

the light of flaring torches, for the moon would rise late, the people saw with wonder and delight the surprise which Brother Francis and Sir John had prepared for them. They looked into a real stable. There was the manger full of hay, there were a live ox and a live ass. Even by torchlight their breath showed in the frosty air. And there, on the hay, lay a dear baby, wrapped from the cold, asleep and smiling. It looked as sweet and innocent as the Christ Child Himself. The people shouted with delight. They clapped their hands and waved their torches.

Then there was silence, for Brother Francis stood before them, and the voice they loved so well, and had come so far to hear, began to read the old story of the birth of the Child Jesus, of the shepherds in the fields, and of the angels' song. When the reading was ended, Brother Francis talked to them as a father might speak to his children. He told of the love that is gentle as a little child, that is willing to be poor and humble as the Baby who was laid in a manger among the cattle. He begged his listeners to put anger and hatred and envy out of their hearts this Christmas Eve, and to think only thoughts of peace and good will.

BROTHER FRANCIS CREATING THE MANGER SCENE
AT GRECCIO

All listened eagerly while Brother Francis spoke, but the moment he finished the great crowd broke into singing. From the church tower the bells rang loud; the torches waved wildly, while voices here and there shouted for Brother Francis and for the Blessed Little Christ. Never before had such glorious hymns nor such joyous shouting been heard in the town of Greccio.

Only the mothers, with babies in their arms, and the shepherds, in their woolly coats, looked on silently and thought: "We are in Bethlehem."

LA VERNA

THE STORY of the Troubadour is almost finished. The last years of his life were years of suffering and sorrow. Now that the brotherhood had grown so large, many of its members were forgetting the teaching of their leader. Instead of serving Lady Poverty, they were serving Lady Wealth, or Lady Pride, or Lady Fame; and they were Little Poor Men only on the outside, in their coarse gray robes and their unshod feet.

97

This change in the Brothers well-nigh broke the heart of Francis of Assisi. He remembered the first winter in the hovel at Rivo Torto, when, in spite of cold and want, the little company had been so happy and so united. He remembered the joy with which they had built the huts in the plain, and had planted their tiny gardens. It seemed to him that his children were scattered far and wide over the world; that they were no longer simple servants of all who needed help, but that each was striving for his own comfort and his own gain.

There came back to him an old dream. He had dreamed of a little black hen who had so many chickens that she could not gather them all under her wings. Some would be left out, to die of cold or to be stolen by the fox. Even in his grief, Francis smiled over his dream. "I am the little hen," he thought, "and I cannot any longer shelter my brood."

Besides his sorrow, Francis had much illness and pain to bear. His body, "Brother Ass," as he sometimes called it, was worn and weak, but his heart was brave, and his spirit was always sweet.

In those days, sick people could not have the help and comfort that doctors and nurses have learned to give. There was no ether nor chloroform to put a patient out of pain, and surgery was horribly cruel. Once when Francis was exceedingly ill, the doctors decided that they must burn his forehead with a hot iron. As the surgeon came close to him with the terrible rod, heated till it looked white and quivering, Francis shrank away fearfully for a minute. Then he lifted his hand and said: "Brother Fire, thou art one of the most beautiful of all things, help me in this hour; thou knowest how I have always loved thee; be courteous to me today."

The Brothers, unable to bear the sight, had gone to the next room. A moment later, they came back, and Francis, smiling on them, asked: "Why did you run away in such a cowardly fashion? I have not felt the pain," he added. "Brother Doctor, if it is necessary, you may begin again."

One great joy remained to Francis almost until the end, the joy of being out of doors. His love for a life under the sky; his love for birds and flowers, for long journeys through the river valleys or among the high mountains, never left him. One mountain he loved best of all. It is called La Verna, and it stands, wild and beautiful, among the Tuscan Apennines. A certain Count Orlando, to whom all the region belonged, had once heard Brother Francis preach, and had said to him: "I have a mountain in Tuscany. It is a silent and lonely place, where one might rest and think and pray. If you would like it, I will gladly give it to you and to your Brothers."

The old story says that Brother Francis was greatly pleased by this gift of the mountain. He thanked first God and then

Messer Orlando, and he promised that when he should return to the Portiuncula he would send some of the Brothers to Messer Orlando, at his castle of Chiusi. This castle stood, and its roofless walls still stand, where the road begins to climb to La Verna.

So it happened, that when Count Orlando went home, he was visited by two Gray Brothers from Assisi, come to see if, in the forest of La Verna, they might find a fit place for Brother Francis. Count Orlando received the two Brothers with the greatest joy and friendliness, and, because the mountain was filled with wild beasts, he sent armed men to escort the strangers. The Little Poor Men, with their guard of soldiers, searched about on the steep, rocky mountain, till they found a small level place, like a natural terrace, looking off to the southwest. "Here," they said, "is the right spot. Let us build huts for ourselves and for our Brothers."

The soldiers of Count Orlando began to cut down great branches from the fir trees and beeches, and, with these, they helped the Brothers to make rude shelters.

Then startled eyes looked out from the green shadows, and soft feet rustled away over the fallen leaves; and a thousand pairs of wings made a whirring sound, for all the wild things of La Verna were disturbed by the loud voices and the ringing axes of Count Orlando's soldiers, and Brother Francis was not there to understand and comfort them.

100

When the green, sweet-smelling huts were finished, the two Brothers with their guard of soldiers went back to the castle of Chiusi to thank Count Orlando for his gift. Then they journeyed down to the plain of Assisi and reported to Brother Francis that the Tuscan mountain was the fittest place in the world in which to think and pray. Brother Francis rejoiced at the account of the two Brothers, and he thought it good that a company of the Poor Men should keep at La Verna the Feast of St. Michael and All Angels, which comes at the end of September.

He started out bravely on foot, as of old, but during the long, rough journey, he became so weak that the Brothers were forced to ask help of a peasant who was riding upon an ass. The peasant gave his beast to the sick man, and walked beside him all the way, until they reached the sheer gray crags below the little huts that Count Orlando's soldiers had built.

Here they rested under an oak tree before making the steep climb. Brother Francis sat looking about the place, of which he had heard so much, and, says the story: "As he was looking and thinking there came great flocks of birds from every direction, singing and beating their wings, and they showed signs of joy and welcome. They circled around Francis, so that some perched on his head, some on his shoulders, on his arms, in his lap and even on his feet.

"His companions and the peasant saw them with wonder, but Francis said, all happy of heart: 'I believe, dearest Brothers, that our Lord Jesus Christ is pleased that we are to live in this lonely mountain, since our sisters and brothers, the birds, show such joy at our coming.'"

The little company lived for some weeks on the mountain. Apart from the others, that he might be more alone, Francis had a tiny hut, and here he spent much time in prayer. Only Brother Leone was allowed to come to him, before dawn each day, bringing his scant food. His only other comrade was a falcon, whose shrill cry used to waken him long before light; but sometimes, when Brother Francis, worn and ill, lay sleeping, Brother Falcon would be silent until later in the morning.

The forest was full of singing birds, but sweeter music than theirs sounded sometimes in the ears of the Little Poor Man. As he grew weaker and weaker in body, Francis fixed his mind more and more on the glory and the joy of the heavenly life.

Once, as he thought on these things, longing to know what heaven might be like, he saw before him a most beau-

BROTHER FRANCIS KNEELING TO PRAY ON HIS
JOURNEY TO LA VERNA

tiful angel with a viol in his left hand and a bow in his right. As Francis gazed, wondering, the angel touched the strings with his bow, and so soft a melody was heard that the spirit of Francis was filled with sweetness. He forgot all his pain of body and mind.

One morning, in the hours before sunrise, Francis was kneeling in prayer not far from his hut, when a light shone in the heaven above him, and came nearer and nearer. Behold! it was a seraph with six wings shining and aflame. As the seraph came nearer in swift flight he seemed to Francis like the figure of a man crucified. Two wings were lifted above his head, and two outstretched in flight and two were folded down, covering all his body. And Francis was filled with fear, and yet with great joy.

Then all the mountain of La Verna seemed to burn with rosiest flame. The flame shone out and lighted the hills and valleys far away, as if it were the red light of dawn. The shepherds, watching their flocks, were frightened to see the mountain all ablaze, and afterward they declared the flame had lasted on La Verna for an hour and more.

The light shone even into the windows of the low houses and little inns in the country round about; so that some mule

BROTHER FRANCIS PRAYING

drivers, who were sleeping at an inn not far away to the west, rose, and saddled and loaded their mules, thinking that it was day. As they went on their journey they were astonished to see the beautiful light fade away over La Verna, and, after an hour of darkness, the real sun rise.

If the shepherds on the hills, and the muleteers going sleepily along the road wondered and feared because of the great light that was not dawn, the Brothers on La Verna wondered still more.

But Brother Francis knew what the vision meant. Often in these last years his life had seemed a failure, and sometimes he had envied the martyrs of the early Church, and even his own Brothers who had given their lives for the faith in Africa and in Spain. Now the vision of pain and glory seemed to say to him: "Be content, Little Poor Man, for not by the martyrdom of thy body, but by the fire of thy spirit, thou art made like to thy Master, Christ."

And the Brothers who wrote down the story tell how, from that wonderful hour upon the mountain, their beloved leader bore on his hands and on his feet marks like the nail-prints of the Crucified.

THE VISION OF THE CRUCIFIXION APPEARING TO
BROTHER FRANCIS

CRUCIFER SERAPINUS SIGNO DOTATE PERTERATIS ANGELICE SINT
SEDES PRE PARATE AVEAZ CVALEX AZELX XINGE AVZAVIE XE

THE TROUBADOUR'S
LAST SONG

ALMOST the first we know of Francis of Assisi is the story of the sweet-voiced lad who sang gay songs of love and war. Almost the last that we know of him is the more beautiful story of the song which he made and sang only a little while before he died. He had been terribly ill, he was weak, and sad, and in great pain, but one morning his friends heard the wonderful voice, strong and clear as of old, singing words that they had never known.

108

He had often sung the sweet old Latin hymns, but these words were Italian, and so simple that it seemed as if the singer made them as he sang. And so he did. The weary, suffering man was still at heart the Troubadour. He was still, as he used to call himself, the Lark, and, like the lark, he sang for sheer happiness and praise. It is not easy to put the quaint old Italian into English; the beauty and the music seem to disappear.

The last song of God's Troubadour, the song that cheered his hours of pain and comforted the friends who loved him, was a "Song of the Sun."

O Lord, we praise Thee for our Brother Sun,
Who brings us day, who brings us golden light.
He tells us of Thy Beauty, Holy One.
We praise Thee, too, when falls the quiet night,
For Sister Moon, and every silver star
That Thou hast set in Heaven, clear and far.

For our brave Brother Wind we give Thee praise;
For clouds and stormy skies, for gentle air;
And for our Sister Water, cool and fair,
Who does us service in sweet, humble ways;
But, when the winter darkens, bitter cold,
We praise Thee every night and all day long.

109

For our good friend, so merry and so bold,
Dear Brother Fire, beautiful and strong.
For our good Mother Earth, we praise Thee, Lord;
For the bright flowers she scatters everywhere;
For all the fruit and grain her fields afford;
For her great beauty, and her tireless care.

It was through this "Song of the Sun" that the last great joy of his life came to Francis. He was the guest of the Bishop of Assisi in the same palace where, so many years before, he had gone with the story of his father's anger and his mother's grief.

Bishop Guido must have been an old man now, and he was, as always, impulsive and hot-tempered. He had kept a certain love for Francis all these years, but with most of his neighbors he was often at odds.

Just now a sharp feud was going on between the Bishop and the Governor of the city, and all Assisi was in tumult. Francis loved his native town, and he loved peace with all his heart, and this quarrel meant to him the deepest sorrow. His days were full of suffering, but he forgot himself, and only prayed that he might make peace between the two men before he died.

One day he called a Brother to him and said: "Go to the

Governor, and beg him to come with all the chief men of the city to the porch before the Bishop's palace." The Governor came at this request from the dying Francis, and when the Bishop stepped out of his palace door he found himself in a gathering of the very men with whom he was at strife.

Just at that moment two Gray Brothers came forward before the two proud enemies, and one said: "My Lords, Brother Francis has made a song for the praise of God, and he begs you will all listen to it," and they began to sing "The Song of the Sun."

They sang the praise of Sun and Moon, of Wind and Fire, of Sister Water and Mother Earth; and then their voices rose higher and sweeter in a new stanza that Francis, in his longing for peace, had added:

> *We praise Thee, Lord, for gentle souls who live*
> *In love and peace, who bear with no complaint*
> *All wounds and wrongs; who pity and forgive;*
> *Each one of these, Most High, shall be Thy Saint.*

The old story tells that the Governor listened, standing humbly "weeping hot tears, for he greatly loved the blessed Francis.

When the song was finished: 'Know in truth,' he said,

111

'that I pardon the Lord Bishop, whom I wish and ought to regard as my lord, for even if someone had murdered my brother, I should be ready to forgive the murderer.'

"After these words he threw himself at the feet of the Bishop and said to him: 'Behold me, ready to do all that you wish, for love of our Lord Jesus Christ and for His servant Francis.'

"Then the Bishop, taking him by the hand, lifted him and said: 'In my calling, I ought to be humble, but since I am by nature too quickly angry, you must pardon me.'"

A few days later Brother Francis was carried out from the Bishop's palace, and borne tenderly down the familiar road toward the Portiuncula. At the Leper Hospital he asked his bearers to halt. He looked back, with dim eyes, lovingly, and, lifting his feeble hand, he blessed Assisi. Then the gray procession entered the forest, and passed softly through the fallen leaves to the poor huts and the bright garden which had been the dearest home of the Brotherhood.

Here the Troubadour, the Little Poor Man, died, happy and high-hearted, singing praise, at the last, for the welcome coming of "Our Sister Death."

THE SISTERS BID FAREWELL TO BROTHER FRANCIS
BEFORE THE CHURCH OF SAINT DAMIANO

IN UMBRIA

Under a roof of twisted boughs
  And silver leaves and noonday sky,
Among gaunt trunks, where lizards house,
  On the hot sunburnt grass I lie;
I hear soft notes of birds that drowse,
  And steps that echo by

Unseen, along the sunken way
  That drops below the city-wall.
Not of today, nor yesterday,
  The hidden, holy feet that fall.
O whispering leaves, beseech them stay!
  O birds, awake and call!

Say that a pilgrim, journeying long,
  From that loud land that lies to west,
Where tongues debate of right and wrong,
  Would be "The Little Poor Man's" guest;
Would learn "The Lark's" divine "Sun Song,"
  And how glad hearts are blest.

Say: "Master, we of overseas
  Confess that oft our hearts are set
On gold and gain; and if, with these,
  For lore of books we strive and fret,
Perchance some lore of bended knees
  And sainthood we forget;

"Still, in one thought our lips are bold—
   That, in our world of haste and care,
Through days whose hours are bought and sold,
   Days full of deeds and scant of prayer,
Of thy life's gospel this we hold:
   Thy hands that toil are fair.

"Therefore, forgive; assoil each stain
   Of trade and hate, of war and wrath;
Teach us thy tenderness for pain;
   Thy music that no other hath;
Thy fellowship with sun and rain,
   And flowers along thy path."

Thou dost not answer. Down the track
   Where now I thought thy feet must pass,
With patient step and burdened back
   Go "Brother Ox" and "Brother Ass."
A mountain cloud looms swift and black,
   O'ershadowing stone and grass.

The silver leaves are turned to gray;
   There comes no sound from hedge nor tree;
Only a voice from far away,
   Borne o'er the silent hills to me,
Entreats: "Be light of heart to-day;
   To-morrow joy shall be."

115

ABOUT THE AUTHOR

Sophie Jewett was a professor of English literature at Wellesley College for many years. She and her sister, who was head of the art department at Mount Holyoke College, often traveled in Europe together. It was on one of these trips that Miss Jewett saw the Giotto frescoes of the life of St. Francis in Assisi, Italy, and was inspired to write this story.

Miss Jewett's family was an old New England one. Her grandfather and great-grandfather founded the town of Moravia; and it was there, in the hilly lake country of central New York, that she grew up. Later she made her home in Buffalo.

ABOUT THE ARTIST

Giotto di Bondone was born in a small village north of Florence, Italy, around 1276. His father was a landowner, and as a boy Giotto tended sheep and cattle in the fields. There is a story that one day the famous painter, Cimabue, discovered him drawing a sheep on a piece of slate with a sharp stone, and took him to be his apprentice.

Wherever Giotto learned his art, he soon became the greatest painter of his time and helped lay the foundation for the Renaissance in Italy. Some of his most famous works are those in honor of St. Francis in the Church of San Francesco in Assisi. After hundreds of years they are unchanged and still singularly beautiful.

Giotto was married and had three sons and three daughters. He was the friend of Dante and Petrarch and was honored and beloved by all the citizens of Florence.

Date Due

MAR 2 1 '59			
JUN 1 8 '67			
NOV 1 8 '69			
AP 13 '70			
Dec 19-73			
NO 23 '87			